Trading Wisd

50 lessons every trader should know

by Cheds

About the Author

I love trading and have been doing it for many years. My formal training is with Japanese candlesticks and classical charting, and I am certified as a CMT (Chartered Market Technician) level 1. My educational background in psychology and brief career as an amateur poker player also guide my approach, paying proper respect to risk management and the study of one's opponent.

On twitter is where I am most well known and can be found @BigCheds. I am also a proud founding analyst at Bitcoin Live, the best in class educational platform for Crypto.

This is my second book. My first published work was a a memoir titled "My Battles with Cancer, a candid patient and caregiver's memoir."

Introduction

My early days of trading were filled with frustration, confusion and constant losses. After making some of the same mistakes over and over again I being to adapt and learned a few tricks to minimize my losses.

As I began passing these tricks on to my fellow traders through my twitter account and blog (chedstrading.blogspot.com) it launched me on a path of learning and teaching. With enough time that path lead to dedicated studies of Japanese candlesticks and classical charting, and ultimately CMT certification.

My career and brand have been built on "helping new traders avoid my old mistakes" and this book is a natural extension of those efforts.

This book is also a natural extension of my "Complete Beginners Guide to Trading" that I wrote back in 2017 when I was undergoing chemotherapy for lymphoma. I subsequently beat my cancer and wrote a book about that experience, and have since continued to grow in my journey as a trader and teacher. Building on my years of work with my twitter account, learning blog and various other writings on trading subjects, I am happy to now bring together in one place all those bits and pieces that have helped to make me a successful trader.

I have personally made every single mistake mentioned in this book multiple times and therefore can speak from the heart, which I hope makes each lesson a little bit easier to learn.

Thank you for reading and best of luck in your trading journey.

Table of contents

TRADING WISDOM

Lesson 1 - Respect your funds

"Treat your money right or it will find a new owner."

I love that quote. It really cuts to the bottom line by reminding us to respect our funds lest they disappear.

In the process of finding good risk/reward opportunities, avoid over exposing yourself when there is no reason to do so.

"In trading, the minute you let your guard down is when the capital destruction begins. Stay vigilant and respect your funds."

An interesting way to think about this is to look at what the average person is willing to spend their funds on. Many refuse to pay for training materials or premium educational sites but have no problem allocating major funds for high risk short term trades.

If you are going to risk large amounts of money you should respect those funds by spending the rather minimal amount it takes to buy a textbook or training service. The money spent in this fashion will have a multiplier effect. As your trading skill improves, your ability to properly utilize your capital will as well and over time that will lead to bigger wins and smaller losses.

Either take trading seriously by studying hard and investing in yourself, or go find a new hobby.

"Always amazes me that some people are willing to risk $50,000++ on speculative trades but refuse to read a trading textbook that might cost $70-$100."

Lesson 2 - What's the rush?

"If you are in a rush to trade, do not be surprised if your money is in a rush to go somewhere else."

Every trade you execute should be well thought out ahead of time. Putting your money to work and risking capital loss is a serious thing and should only be done with a clear plan in mind. That plan should include a trading thesis and stop loss.

When you rush into your trades you are prone to making simple mistakes. How often have you entered a long position and smiled as the price went up, only to find out you hit the wrong button and went short? How many times have you entered a trade and bought far more or far less than you intended by mistake? Going too fast and clicking the wrong button can lead to disaster, so always take a deep breath and go slow when you enter a trade.

"Most of the time in these bottoming situations I lose money when I fool around throwing in bids before any type of bottoming pattern has even started to form. Wait for things to settle down and identify a solid idea that you can use as your fail point."

I have found that it is difficult to stay away from trading when I think something is in the process of bottoming. When this happens an incredible urge to jump in to the action comes over me. Since I do not want to miss that perfect entry I scale into every minor bottoming formation I see only to get stopped out minutes later.

This happens over and over, when in the end if I had just waited for a while I could have played a clear bottom forming pattern when the price action offered a more clear signal. More times than not the bottom is slow to form, so there is plenty of time to jump in on a support re-test, diagonal break or horizontal break.

"My best advice is to follow momentum. Don't be fancy and try to anticipate when it is going to turn around."

Momentum has a way of making itself clear if you are willing be observant and look for clues in the price action about when the trend is changing.

Traders talk about "catching falling knives", referring to this process of anticipating a bottom before it has formed. Messing around and trying to catch falling knives will shred your bankroll, unless you are a pro.

"If you are going to throw some serious funds at something, at least do yourself a favor and take a look at the chart first."

Another way of rushing into a trade is buying without even

looking at the chart. Sometimes you see an idea in a chat room or news article that catches your attention and makes you feel the instant need to open a new position. No matter what you should look at the chart and try to understand the direction of the trend, as well as where you are buying in relation to major support and resistance.

Buying blindly leads to playing from behind, with one mistake leading to another and all of a sudden you have a big problem on your hands.

"Remember folks, it's a marathon not a sprint so pace yourself."

Lesson 3 - Stay calm under pressure

"In many ways the difference between success and failure comes down to staying calm under pressure. Do not panic."

To be a profitable trader you must stay cool under pressure so that you can take advantage of bargain basement prices when they come around. When everyone else is panicking you are scaling in to your position because your low ball bid filled.

With the comfort of this excellent entry you are now watching the order flow to decide if you want to add more or wait for a bit and see how it plays out. It is nice to have options.

When panic hits the market it is time for you to go to work because other people are making bad decisions, allowing you the opportunity to capitalize.

"The next time $BTC #Bitcoin drops $10,000 in a day (and it will) try to remember that is a buying opportunity, not a panicking opportunity."

Executing this strategy correctly will take a lot of practice but the pay off is worth it. The ability to stay calm when the market is blood red will help you to spot favorable risk/reward setups developing in an otherwise hectic environment. When the price pulls back so far that it is dipping below the lower bands or perhaps re-visiting that prior breakout level, you strike. These favorable scenarios give us confidence when others are paralyzed by fear and unable to pull the trigger.

"If you are a bull then pullbacks are your best friend. The more we digest, the higher we go."

How many times have you studied a chart and come up with a great plan for entering on a retracement, but as soon as it happens you get nervous and change your mind? I've been there myself in the past but now I stick with my plan, trust myself and see the idea all the way through.

These larger market draw downs offer us the opportunity to buy dips in established up-trends, which is a great way to build up your portfolio.

"If you loved these alts 5 minutes ago, you should ADORE them after a 10-20% haircut. Stop chasing the green and learn to love the red. It is valentines day after all."

Lesson 4 - Wait for opportunity

"I do not know who needs to hear this but: You do not have to be in a trade every second. It is okay to watch and wait for a really good opportunity."

It is important to avoid the need to be in something all the time, as that will just get you in to trouble. Instead why not just casually watch the price action while you wait for a really good spot? That leads to another question, how can you do that and still stay connected to the price action to take advantage of an opportunity when it comes around?

One way is to set low ball bids ahead of time. Place these orders so low in fact that you do not think they have a shot at filling. Then set an alert on your phone or trading software to tell you when the price gets close by and go for a walk.

The difference between a forced trade and a real opportunity is not always easy to see when you are in the moment, but patience will help you spot the difference. Over time you will find that you can get some really nice entries by waiting rather than forcing the action.

"Stop trying to predict what is going to happen next and observe, you just might learn something."

You want to watch out for the need to instantly put your cash to work once you take profit or trim a losing position. Funds sitting idly in your trading account should not be the reason for the trade. Rather the reason should be a clear and defensible trading opportunity based on a clean thesis. Examples of this are revisiting broken resistance, testing the lower range of a prior reversal candle or the confirmed break of some consolidation pattern that resolves in the direction of the primary trend.

"Sometimes doing nothing is the hardest trade, but is often the best trade."

It can be really frustrating to sit around and wait for a good trading setup, especially when you are sitting on a pile of cash. When you are in these moments remind yourself that it is better to miss a move than to get in at the wrong time. Keep in mind that when you wait for confirmation of your trading thesis, you are giving yourself a better chance to profit from the trade.

"In poker, you don't have to play every hand, you learn a lot by watching. Same for trading - avoid the FOMO, sit back and observe the action instead."

Trading is similar to poker in the sense that it is tempting to enter a new play just to cure your boredom. When you sit down at the table with a big pile of chips you get a rush from anticipating the action to come. While you dream of big gains in a short period of time, the combination of liquidity and boredom make it tempting to jump into a new play just for some quick action. Avoid the urge to kill time this way and instead follow the proper strategy of sitting back and waiting for good risk/reward setups.

> *"Boredom is not a good enough reason to trade - Wait for opportunity."*

We all get bored when trading, so it is important to ask yourself if you are making a trade because the setup is favorable or are you making the trade because you are itching for action. Start to correct this error by observing your own behavior.

A great way to prevent this boredom trading is to use strict criteria for entering a trade, and only initiating a position if all those conditions are met. If this method does not work here is a fail-safe system to intentionally slow yourself down before entering a trade.

When you are ready to initiate a new trading position grab a pen and paper and write down your trade idea. Explain to yourself and any other reader why you think you should open the trade. Go for a quick jog or maybe take some time on the exercise bike or even go for a swim, and then come back with a clear head and read what you wrote down previously. If after re-reading your trade idea it still makes sense then you can enter the trade.

"An opportunity is something you know when you see it, everything else is a forced trade."

Another good way to keep from over trading is to force yourself to have a certain amount of cash on hand at all times. Always keeping a certain % of your trading portfolio in cash is a great way to make sure you are ready to take advantage of opportunities when they come along. It also has the added benefit that the remaining percentage of your active trading funds will have to be used more selectively so that you do not run out of cash.

"If your entry sucks you are going to play catch up the whole time and probably make more mistakes. Focus on low ball entries to make things easier on yourself."

Lesson 5 - Go easy on yourself

"It is important to have a short memory and forgive yourself for poor trading decisions in the past. The alternative is bankroll ruin from a self fulfilling prophecy of failure."

There is no shortcut to becoming a good trader, you must put in the time and effort to get there. Along the way you will make the mistakes that will ultimately form the foundation of your trading style and philosophy. By suffering from these mistakes you can learn what not to do, and as such are able to develop a more effective trading instinct.

If you are just getting started you do not have the luxury of that experience, so really making mistakes is the only way to learn.

"Step one in trading is to survive your mistakes."

After a big loss it is easy to get down on yourself, which leads to a loss of confidence. As this process plays out, failure becomes a self fulfilling process.

To avoid developing this bad habit give yourself enough time to both make mistakes and learn from them. Survive and stay in the game so you can learn to become a successful trader.

Sometimes you make a mistake so bad that all you want is to get back to even. Deep in the red you swear up and down that you

19

will never make this mistake again, promising to learn your lesson. If you do eventually get out of that mess remember this feeling and do not let it go.

"Just because you played the last trade poorly doesn't mean you have to play the next trade poorly - Learn from your mistakes but do not let them haunt you."

Lesson 6 – Experience comes first

"Knowing the rules is what gets you to the table. Experience is what keeps you at the table as you manage risk and wait for good opportunities."

The best way to stay "at the table" is to properly manage your funds based on an understanding of the risk/reward offered by each type of trading setup. How does one develop the ability to discern where true value lies? The answer is through the study of classical charting, Japanese candlesticks, Elliot waves or other methods of technical analysis.

With some hard work and dedicated practice you too can learn how to understand the ebb and flow of price action.

"The minute you stop learning is the minute you give up on yourself."

Most people start out trading as a hobby and have a high expectation of losing money. They may have some hope of getting lucky and winning, but know that they lack the experience required to trade as a professional would.

After picking up a few tricks here and there some of these new traders decide to take this hobby to the next level by studying hard and by practicing over and over.

When you think about your time away from the physical process of trading, how much effort are you exerting to improve your craft? Are you studying textbooks and watching educational videos on technical analysis? Are you taking time out of the weekend to identify key chart price levels for the following week's action?

"If you survive a bad trading mistake then you have paid for that lesson. Don't let it go to waste."

Whether it be technical knowledge or proper risk management strategies that you are lacking, you should never be afraid to ask for the help you need. Put in the work to improve your craft, taking advantage of the many great people and organizations out there that are willing to help you.

On the other hand having all the best teachers and learning materials available will mean almost nothing if you do not put in the effort it takes to succeed.

Over time your results will be your body of work. Push yourself as hard as you can to survive and thrive as a trader.

"No skill worth having can be achieved without practice. That includes trading."

Lesson 7 - Keep grinding

"If you quit now you'll never know how close you came to quitting before you made it."

I know it may seem a little confusing, but if you quit now you will never know how close you came to giving up before you ultimately became a successful trader.

There are so many things that can go wrong and make you want to give up trading. Most of them come after breaking basic rules like always using a stop loss or never investing more than 10% of your bankroll in any one play. When it seems like nothing is going your way, pulling all your money out and walking away feels like a great way to end the pain. However, if you do this and give up on your trading career you are proving your doubters right, the ones who told you that you did not have what it takes to succeed.

"The minute you give up is the minute your doubters win. Prove them wrong."

We all respond to criticism and doubt differently. Many of us use it as encouragement because we know that we *are* good enough and can succeed. The fact that someone else doubts us is a great motivator as we want to prove them wrong. Not only that but we want them to feel bad because we became successful despite everything they said.

Other people respond to doubt by giving up, believing that they really do not have what it takes to succeed. How do you know if you actually have what it takes or not?

"You will never know what you are capable of until you try. Prove the doubters wrong!"

Give yourself a chance to make it and prove your detractors wrong. The road may be long and filled with disappointment but in the end it will be worth it. Keep on grinding.

"Keep grinding! Don't let anyone tell you that you can not get to where you want to be."

Lesson 8 - Don't marry your bags

"If you feel like you need to defend every negative comment you see about a play you are holding, that would suggest an unhealthy level of emotional connection. Be surgical with your investments rather than falling in love with them."

Trust me I have been here about a million times before. More so in my early days of trading than now, but as soon as I had a larger than average position size I became attached to that play. When the market was closed I scanned the message boards and twitter feeds to see what people were saying about it, and if I saw something bad I would jump into action and defend the company as if I were defending my own personal reputation.

"Emotions are great when you are painting or writing or composing music, but when you are trading they are kryptonite."

These emotional manifestations can cause problems in many ways, such as after a failed trade. Losing money is frustrating because you thought you had a good plan and then everything fell apart. Maybe you made a tactical error or just got unlucky, but either way it did not work out. Emotionally compromised, now you want to chase after that loss and redeem yourself so you jump right back into that failed ticker. More often than not this trade will also end badly, as you do not have a good feel for the price action and one mistake tends to lead to another.

Another way to get in trouble is after a taking profit from a winning trade that keeps going up after you sell. Now you are frustrated and get mad at yourself, and mad at the play for not going down immediately after you sold.

Because of this grudge you now hold, in the future you will miss out on new opportunities that come along all because you did not make the perfect trade last time. It does not mater if this play offers you another great entry, you will remember that you missed out last time and just can not get over it.

"Avoid the impulse to let one bad trade ruin your day. Stay focused and reject the emotion and self loathing."

Lesson 9 - Profit taking

"When you are so excited about your trade that you take a screen shot to send to your buddy, that is probably when you should sell."

One of the hardest things to do is learn how and when to take profit. When you are in something that is up-trending it is tempting to just let your position ride to see if it can turn in to a home-run. On the other hand, if you do not sell near resistance/supply the price might drop quickly and then your trade becomes a hold, something you were hoping to avoid.

A general rule that most advanced traders follow is that you should scale in and scale out of each position, so as you approach a major resistance there is nothing wrong with trimming some profits. If the price dips you can add some back, and if not you still have a core position to take advantage of any continued momentum.

"Taking profit along the way makes all future decisions easier."

Every time you take profit on a trade your remaining position is smaller and that makes each future decision easier. Now there is less pressure because any action you take represents a smaller percentage of your risk assets.

Remember that it is okay to miss out on that extra 5 or 10% in profit because timing the exact top and bottom are extremely difficult to the point of being impossible. In addition to making your future decisions easier, you are also lessening your exposure to holding a risky asset when you take profit. Depending on the market and security there is always a chance that trading can be suspended, or that some news event shocks the market and causes serious damage to the price.

On the other hand you must strike a balance with taking profit too soon by staying connected to the price action. Trading wisdom teaches us that we should be following the trend as long as is profitable, all the while looking for signs of weakening.

It is also important not to completely close out winning trades at the first sign of trouble like a 15 minute reversal candle or RSI getting hot. To avoid getting faked out too easily you need some type of a multi level confirmation filter that requires some follow through on a signal, such as a close below a key level rather than just a candle wick.

Though it is a balancing act I would personally lean towards more aggressive profit taking than not, because you will never go broke that way.

"If you are up big now, maybe take a little off the table. You can never go broke by taking profit."

Lesson 10 - Emotional mindfulness

"Any trade that makes you feel uncomfortable should be closed immediately."

This is something that took me a while to figure out, but once I did I realized that I had been improperly sizing my trading positions. There is no set rule for how big your position should be or even exactly how aggressively to scale into it. Each trader must decide based on their own trading style, risk tolerance and personal needs. In the quest to find that perfect balance you should pay attention to your emotional mind-state as you add risk.

"If buy something and immediately feel uncomfortable, you probably have too much money in that play."

Now you are so uncomfortable with your position that it is hard to take your eyes of the screen. Every tick up or down makes you sweat, because you have committed more money than you can afford to lose and can not figure out how to get out of this mess.

One way to alleviate this problem is to only play with money you can afford to lose. That way when you get into these tough situations it is easier to remain calm and minimize the damage to your bankroll.

Another way to stop this cycle is to take a break from trading and let things settle down for a bit. Often when we become too

29

involved with something we lose perspective and make mistakes we would not otherwise make. After some time to decompress you will be in a much better position to re-enter the fight with your wits about you. Talk a walk and shed that emotional baggage.

"Trading without mindfulness is pure gambling."

More times than not what we visualize and think about tends to happen, so with that in mind you should envision yourself doing well and succeeding in your trading life. Be your own best friend rather than your own worst enemy, and give yourself a chance to do well. Negative thinking is toxic and self fulfilling.

"If you enter a trade thinking you are going to lose money, then chances are you will lose money. Be mindful of your mood / confidence level. If you are unable to visualize success, sit out the trade."

Lesson 11- Be ready to buy the fear

"Everyone wants a pullback until it actually comes."

This is an extremely critical lesson because it affects so many of us. When the price is moving up quickly and enthusiasm is extremely high, all we want is pullback so we can add some more shares with confidence.

Then once the price breaks support and starts to go lower we start to panic and are not sure if we want to buy anymore. Not only that but we are now thinking about selling, and are mad that we did not take profit at "the top". How can we end this cycle of reactive trading?

When the market is in free fall mode and it feels like everyone is giving up left and right, that is usually a great time to add some exposure. This is a favorable environment as you want to be following the general rule of buying the blood and selling the greed.

"One of the hardest things to do is train yourself to buy weakness, rather than selling in to it."

Through your technical analysis studies you know that it is a great strategy to buy dips in up-trends. That is the voice in the back of your mind that keeps you calm, knowing that you are buying weakness in a strong chart.

"Buy when no one else wants it, sell when everyone else wants it."

It is important to avoid the cycle of buying the top and selling the bottom. If you find yourself constantly chasing tickers that are moving and then easily giving up after some consolidation, then you are going to watch your bankroll evaporate.

You need to factor in the psychology of the market before deciding what to do with your trade. Most often when people are giving up and sentiment is low the price reflects a value, and if you scoop in you are likely grabbing a distressed asset at lower than fair value. Always keep some extra cash just in-case a big price drops happen on one of your favorite plays, and buy that dip with confidence.

"I am sensing some fear in the market - That means you should have cash ready in case we get any kind of flash dip."

Lesson 12 - Define your risk

"Best way to avoid these situations is to properly define your risk. DEFINE IT. Do that by setting a stop loss and refusing to add to your losing trades. Set limits and stick with them because it is the big losers that take you out of this game."

One of the keys to surviving this game we call trading is to define your risk at every available opportunity. That means limiting your position size, taking profit at major resistance or even waiting for a better entry. How actively and carefully you define your risk will have major implications on the long term health of your bankroll.

One really bad habit that you should try to avoid is refusing to sell for a loss. I know from personal experience how hard a habit this is to break, as well as how harsh the penalty can be for having it. The bottom line is that you need to cut your losers before they destroy your trading account.

I cannot tell you how many times as a trader I have refused to sell for a small loss and it blew up in my face. When I looked at my brokerage account and hit refresh, seeing that position in red made me feel uncomfortable and because of that I was unwilling to sell. Selling would have made the loss permanent so I held on in the hopes I could turn things around. What happened next? That small loss turned into a massive loss.

I was too stubborn to sell and take my medicine, and instead of selling I stood there frozen in panic.

"Refusing to take a small loss will often lead to the opportunity to refuse to take a big loss."

How do you avoid getting stuck in this position? Start with a trading plan and stick to that plan, which of course includes using a stop loss based on your trading thesis or idea.

Once your trade is sufficiently in profit, moving your stop loss up to a break-even or better level is a great way to remove the stress and anxiety that comes from holding that position. This strategy works great for me, as I like to be "free-riding" as soon as possible. Of course you could counter that I am likely losing out on some gains, but I am okay with that as I like to define my risk, and with that my stress level as well.

"Moving your stop loss into profit is a great way to reduce your stress level towards zero."

Lesson 13 - Manage your stack

"Scale in at support, scale out at resistance, have a tight logical stop loss and the rest is pure luck."

Another central concept of risk management is proper bankroll usage.

One common practice is to limit each play or trade to a certain % of your total portfolio, perhaps 1-5%. By doing so you are not placing too much emphasis on any one trade idea, because the consequences can be disastrous. This is especially the case if you are trading volatile markets. In theory a diversified basket of risky assets would serve you better if you are trading in that type of market.

"I coach to all successful traders to cap their trading account at a certain number and transfer out profits every week/month. That way you are less tempted to ape up the risk threshold."

Managing the connection between your bankroll (trading account) and your bank account is also important. If your trading account is too large from a series of wins, take some of that extra profit and transfer it out to your bank account. There are multiple benefits to this strategy: Firstly taking out the money makes it feel real and locks up the gains, and secondly limiting you trading account size limits your volatility.

Generally speaking your goals should be humble, and your approach to reaching them methodical.

Start small with the goal of making one 5% winner this week, and go from there. If you do not reach that goal, examine your methodology and record it in a trading log and journal for analysis. If you do make your goal perhaps move your target up to 7%, or try to make two 5% winners the following week.

Take an incremental approach, and slowly adjust your goals as you go along, tweaking here and there as you learn what works and what does not.

Rather than trying to grow your account from $5,000 to $50,000 overnight, approach trading with more modest goals based on your experience, and factoring in mistakes you expect to make in pursuit of your goals. Remember to pay attention to each step along the way as you are learning, because in the end that is what will make you a winning trader.

"One decent trade can make up for 10 failed trades if you properly manage your stop losses. You don't need home runs in this game. Singles, stolen bases and sac flies are good enough."

Lesson 14 - Pick your spots carefully

"If you are not making money in this market chances are that are you trying to fight the trend - Trade WITH the trend, not against it."

My biggest trading losses come when I enter in the middle of the channel, rather than buying on a support re-test or shorting at resistance. That "no-trade zone" you hear about is real, so if you respect it your wallet will thank you.

I could have easily worked this in to the lesson on patience and waiting for the bottom to form, but I feel the "position in channel" of your entry deserves a lesson of its own. That is how important it is to your chances of pulling off a winning trade.

"Follow the price action - Once it tells you where supply and demand lay, pay attention."

When the price is consolidating in a well defined range such as a rectangle, symmetrical triangle or even a flag pattern there is an upper and lower boundary that the price seems to be respecting. One of the basic rules of classical charting is that you should not trade against the trend, so in a bull flag you should be looking to go long at the bottom of the channel, rather than looking for spots to short at the top of that channel.

Why? Because the primary or natural trend is up in this case there is a higher chance that the price will break up and resume the trend. This is even more so the case if the pattern is mature (has been developing for a while). You want to either buy at the bottom of the flag, or buy on the break out so you can use that level as your stop loss. Buying in the middle of the channel will get you in to trouble.

The same can be said for during a downtrend when the price is consolidating in some type of sideways range like a bear rectangle. You want to initiate your short at the top of that range (resistance), rather that right at the bottom of that range (support), or in the middle of the channel. Sell the strength in a downtrend as it is a move against the primary trend.

The overall point here is that you want to be initiating your position at the correct position in the channel so that you have the best shot to turn that trade into some profit. If you miss the ideal entry be disciplined and wait for the next correct entry, rather than jumping in and buying in the "middle" of the channel.

"Never buy in the middle of the channel. Either short at resistance, buy at support. There are so many different things to play/ways to play them so you should be selective."

Lesson 15 - Stick with what works

"Cut your losers, add to your winners and the rest is history."

It may sound simple, but it is true. If you find yourself unwilling to add to losing trades and preferring to add to your winning trades the chances are that you are a winning trader.

Everyone has heard of the phrase "averaging down", but how about "averaging up"? When your trade turns green and breaks some resistance or support level confirming your trade thesis that is a good time to "average up" and increase your position size. Because you have already correctly picked the direction of the trade, it is advantageous for you to increase your risk amount and ride the trend. This way you will reap the rewards of continuation.

Averaging down is okay if done in certain ways, such as when you have scaled in lightly beforehand and this new entry offers an even greater risk/reward type of scenario.

Much of proper trading strategy involves following and capturing the benefit of momentum, so if you think about it that way it makes sense to add to positive momentum plays and reduce risk exposure to negative ones.

If you cut your losing plays early there will be less pressure on your winning plays to make up for those big trading mistakes. This is a key component to any sustainable trading strategy. As you examine the chart on those plays you are holding, make sure you have that level marked where you would "average up" in addition to where you would cut your position.

"It's okay to be wrong more than you are right, as long as you cut your losers and add to your winners."

Lesson 16 - Switch time-frames wisely

"A great analogy for trading off the 5 minute chart is driving while completely drunk - You might make it home but eventually it will catch up with you."

Low time frame trading can be fun because we get to see rapid price movements and have the chance to nail the absolutely perfect entry. That being said, the quality of the signals you are getting at this low a time frame is quite poor. Why is that?

The general rule in classical charting is that the longer the time frame, the stronger the signal. This is true because with a longer time frame the price action is less sensitive to intraday trading moves and is more so a function of the primary trend.

"Think about your chart time frames like a scientist using a microscope. You need to move around the magnification until things come into focus, comfortable with each time frame so you can process each signal in its own context."

So that begs the question. How do we know what time frame to use?

If you find that you are having trouble correctly reading the signals your best bet is to move to a higher time frame. Let the 4 hour chart become a 6 or 12 hour, or even switch from daily to weekly if that is your style of trading. Rather than zooming in you should be inclined to zoom OUT and take in the bigger picture. Once you have the primary trend figured out, you can move to lower time frames when the price is at key support or resistance levels.

Additionally, one thing to keep in mind as you move around the time frames is that you should be careful not to keep changing them to justify your directional bias. To avoid this mistake you should be consistent in your approach to trade examination, using a standard time frame to generate trading ideas.

"You can look at any time frame, just as a general rule the longer the time frame the stronger the signal."

Lesson 17 – Don't fight the trend, ride it

"The investor or trader should never attempt to anticipate a reversal, but rather should wait for the actual reversal and then act with the comfort of trading with the new trend."

A fundamental law of technical analysis is that you should wait for a clear signal to appear and then act on it. Do not get cute trying to guess where the exact bottom lies. Instead wait for a signal to clearly define itself and then deploy your funds with the benefit of the trend at your back.

So how do we know when the bottom is in? What should we be looking for to know when the trend has reversed? First of all you want to watch out for volume. We typically see the most volume at the top and the bottom of a chart as the bulls and bears battle for control of the momentum.

In a downtrend you will be able to spot a falling resistance trend line that any future bounce can be measured against. As the price will make a series of lower highs on attempted bounces you can mark those levels as potential momentum turning points.

Perhaps most important to any reversal is a higher low, the real first step towards generating a bounce.

The way a higher low forms can be explained psychologically. Once we all agree that bottom has been put in, our greed kicks in and want it to dip back there again so we can load, this time with confidence of the trend reversal in our favor. As the price approaches this level again the buyers get anxious, and fearing that they might miss out they move their bids up and the higher low forms.

"My best advice to you is to follow momentum. Don't be fancy and try to anticipate when it is going to turn around."

Lesson 18 - Stay focused

"Having 10 or 15 plays at once does not mean you are going to make 10 or 15 times the amount of money. More than likely you are going to lose focus, screw it up and make nothing."

While you are risking serious money you should take the process equally seriously and that means keeping an eye on the chart where your funds are now parked. If you have too many plays opened at once, you are likely going to miss out on the important clues that the price action is giving you.

Anything that requires watching should have clear chart levels marked out that would lead you to either raise or lower your risk amount. If you are distracted by watching something else you may miss a key signal and that can be extremely costly.

"If you are having trouble trading my advice would be to focus on fewer plays. Reduce your watch-list to 10 or less, and learn the ins and outs of their price action. When a ticker/symbol becomes "familiar" your instincts kick in."

Having too many charts up at once is not the only way to get distracted while trading.

What if you decide to enter a trade while you are watching your favorite sports game with some friends. Minutes later you get wrapped up in the game and forget to watch the chart and while you were away it broke a key support level and dropped 10%. What a disaster!

"If you treat trading like a hobby chances are you will be looking for a new hobby soon."

Watching sports while trading is not the only way to get in trouble. You can also get in trouble trading while you are drinking, or doing drugs. When you have money in play you should treat it with respect and that means staying sober so that you have the best chance possible to pull off a winning trade.

In my view another way people get distracted is by focusing too much on long term price predictions. When you are thinking about where the price might go in the future, you are taking your focus away from what is happening in the moment, which makes you more likely to miss some clues from the price action.

"Stop trying to predict what price your favorite play is going to be at the end of the year and pay attention to what it is telling you now about the supply/demand dynamic. Less predicting, more observing."

Lesson 19 – Sell and move on

"Cutting failed trade positions not only frees up trading capital, it also frees up mental capital. Holding on to and watching your red positions is an emotional drain."

Have you ever had the experience of selling and as soon as the order goes through you feel regret and worry? Maybe you made the wrong decision and left a lot of profit on the table, or perhaps you are worried that the small loss you took would have turned around into a nice gain.

Now smack dab in the middle of the trading day you have to stop everything else you are doing and watch that one stupid play to make sure it really does go the way you thought it would when you sold. Every time it ticks the wrong way you feel miserable, and when it corrects that you feel better again, mired in a constant state of emotional distress.

"If you spend your time obsessing over old losses you have a high probability of generating new ones."

One mistake I see a lot of people making (That I have made myself many times) is after a big loss - Thinking you have to make that money back in the same play - This is a bad idea as you do not have a good feel for the trade and are likely to repeat the same mistakes that cost you money in the first place. More times than not is it better to move on to something fresh, without all the baggage that comes from double dipping into a failed play.

Every new trade offers you the opportunity to apply your skills and turn them into profit, but if you are still licking your wounds from the last play the odds are stacked against you.

"When I close out a losing trade I delete that ticker/symbol from my watch-list so that I am not tempted to jump back in and "chase after" the money I lost. Go make that money back in something fresh and clean, and preferably uptrending."

Lesson 20 - Trust your first instinct

"If you look at a chart and can not figure out which way it is going in the first few moments, move on. Find a clear signal."

I am a strong believer in the idea that when you first look at at chart you should have a good feeling of which way it is going. If you can not tell, that means the chart has mixed signals and you should move on to something else that can give you a cleaner "read". So much of what determines our profit and loss is how selective we are with our entries, so with that in mind you should find a trade setup that is clear to you as soon as you set your eyes upon it.

If that is the case then the natural next question is how does one learn to have that gut feeling, or develop that "muscle memory" to know what a good and bad chart look like at first glance? As discussed in other lessons there are key components to any downtrend reversal, such as a higher low and then lower high break.

In addition you can see the strength in a chart that continues to put in a series of higher lows and higher highs, as well as displaying strong volume on breakouts. Or perhaps you see that the price is now visiting a key level that has served as support many times in the past, and decide that this might be set up for a nice trade with a tight stop loss.

Either way after a good amount of time and practice you will learn to get a sense of what you are looking at be it uptrend, downtrend or sideways chop.

"Gut feeling is underrated. The thing is it only comes with experience and by watching the chart hours and hours a day."

Lesson 21 - Dangers of social media

"If you are watching more chats than charts your system is broken."

Chat rooms are good but if you are generating all your trade ideas from there it is really easy to end up headed in the wrong direction. Using chat rooms as a primary source of trade ideas leaves you dependent on others, with the blind hope that they have picked something good for you to risk your hard earned money on.

It is possible that you have found a good chat room with veteran traders, but what if it is just a pump and dump group? Sure you might get lucky on the first or second play, but you never know when the people running that group are going to dump on you and that is a real problem. Following a paid group leader's calls can work out sometimes, but there is no real accountability if things go wrong and you are left holding the bag. If you can learn to find plays on your own then you can hold yourself accountable and learn a great deal in the process.

"You can feel the hundreds of thousands of people scouring message boards and social media right now to try and find comfort from the posts of others to feel better about red positions. I get it... my comfort comes from candles and lines on charts."
@chartguys on Twitter

So many of us do it. As soon as we find ourselves in a tough trading situation we run to social media to to comfort ourselves with the words of like-minded individuals. We do this because we are not confident enough in our current trading plan so we look to others for confirmation.

It is quite natural to get caught up listening to people on social media who tell you that whatever play you are in will keep going and try to discourage you from taking profit. How many times have you heard "This is the last time X will be priced this low"?

The real truth is that the best traders are the ones who are honest and say that they have no idea what is going to happen next, yet are prepared to trade whatever scenario comes their way.

"The best traders will admit that they have no idea what is about to happen next. Treat anyone who claims otherwise with a degree of caution."

You should never be so impressionable that by simply seeing a tweet or chat room message you are encouraged to open a new trade and risk your funds. All your trades should be planned out well ahead of time, and if not you should spend some time watching the price action before bidding.

Well you might ask, what is the problem with listening to people on twitter who seem to be sending out winning plays? The problem here is that these folks are only showing you their best stuff, and are hiding their losers so you that get a distorted image of their trading skill.

"Never execute a trade based on a single tweet or message you see from someone else. Be a rock, not a blade of grass blowing in the wind."

You have to find a way to avoid the "shiny object" trade. Imagine you are having a tough trading week and all of a sudden you see a certain play being mentioned by everyone. It is tempting to stop what you are doing and immediately jump in to this play as a way to fix your "bad trading day", but in reality you are being incredibly irresponsible. Avoid chasing that shiny object, and instead stick with what you have been watching.

"It is okay not to chase every play you see on twitter. Stay focused on your own watch-list, and be the master of your plays."

Lesson 22 - Buy the rumor, sell the news

"Things always rise in anticipation. That's why it's buy the rumor sell the news. The run already happened."

This ties back into the general concept we have touched on in a few lessons already in regards to buying weakness and selling strength. This applies when there is a future catalyst that everyone knows about.

If you notice much of the time you will see a steady price rise leading up to this event, as people load up in anticipation of the beginning of a massive uptrend. Other people may not even be paying attention, and on the day of that big event they see in the news that something is happening which tempts them to jump in and ride the momentum.

The problem here is that much of the price gains are already baked in, because for many weeks of time that day's events were already known. As a result of this fore knowledge the market drove the price up to a price it believed was correct based on the value of that news event.

After the news comes out the price begins to fall and all those people who bought weeks ago start taking profit. Then after some period of time the price drifts back down to where it started before the news was even rumored, and the cycle is complete.

Any time you are thinking about placing a trade based on some news driven event, ask yourself if you are buying in anticipation of the event or based on the event itself happening. Ride the way up and take profit as soon as the date arrives, if not just beforehand.

"Always ask yourself. Am I buying the rumor, or am I buying the news?"

Lesson 23 - Trading journal

"If you find yourself constantly selling the bottom and buying the top, record in a journal how you are feeling/what you are thinking at the time of trade execution and then look back on that later for a bit of mindfulness training."

What if you keep repeating these old mistakes? Why is that so easy to do? Trading technique is like muscle memory and when you have repeated the same mistakes over and over it is in your nature to repeat these mistakes. The first step in ending this horrible cycle is to be aware of your mistakes through mindfulness trading and using a trading journal.

A trading journal is a great way to give yourself the opportunity to learn from your mistakes, and more importantly a way to keep yourself honest. With this journal you should state your rationale behind each trade, what your trading plan will be for taking profit as well as a stop loss level based on a clearly defined thesis or trade idea.

"Keep a trading journal. Write down your winning trades, your losing trades and even the ones you don't take. Over time you will learn something as you analyze your trading behaviors and spot your bad habits. Keep yourself honest because no one else is going to."

While you are in the trade write down how you are feeling and what you are thinking, more or less observing your own behavior as you enter and watch the trade. Then after you close out the trade it is important to go back and record the results, as well as what you are thinking at the moment you sell. By recording your thoughts and feelings right at the critical decision time you are able to go back later and objectively analyze the trade without letting your current emotions or bias get in the way.

Big losses should be recorded in red, underline and bold, and maybe even larger font so that they stick out when you open the journal each time. This way you do not make it so easy to ignore your mistakes, otherwise what is the point of the exercise?

In addition to your trading journal make sure to keep a "trading log". A trading log is similar to a journal but with one big difference. In this case you use an excel spreadsheet to log your entry, exit and profit and loss from each trade. You can also track the fees you pay, how frequently you are trading and pretty much anything else you can put down in number form.

At the end of the day or the week you should analyze your wins and losses to look for information about what is working and what is not working, as the numbers are now in black and white (and red) so they are hard to ignore. Tally up your wins and losses to see how you did, and compare that to prior weeks, and over time you will build up a strong data set.

"Trading is a brutal game guys - start small, paper trade, keep a journal and study your mistakes. Learn the ebb and flow before risking big $$$."

Holding yourself accountable can be hard when you are your own boss.

If you are only focusing on your winning trades and ignoring losses that will end up destroying your bankroll. You need to find some way to hold yourself accountable so you can stay on track.

Some people use weekly/monthly goals, or even a public social media account where they post wins and losses. Create a structure by which you can benchmark your results and hold yourself accountable, that way you will remain focused on eliminating repeat mistakes.

Do whatever it takes to survive your mistakes and stay in the game.

"Step 1 in trading is to survive your mistakes."

Lesson 24 - Addiction to gambling

"Am I the only one who finds it calming to just stare are a chart and watch the candles form? Oh wait, that's addiction."

We all know how addictive gambling can be, almost to the point where you are never satisfied no matter how much of a thrill you achieve. Once you get a taste of that the rush that comes from looking at a big brokerage account or trading position, your whole attitude changes and you want to feel that way over and over again.

Gambling addiction leads to the feeling that you must be in a play at all times. You feel the need to make a move no matter what, and often end up forcing the action to satisfy those needs.

What are some of the signs that you might have a problem?

If you find yourself waking up at 3 AM and making hastily unplanned trades, then that is a problem. If you find yourself trading from your phone while you are on the toilet, trading while not sober or trading while casually hanging out on the couch and not doing any serious chart analysis first, then that is a problem.

Trading recklessly with a big position is also a clear sign that you have a problem. If your need to feel the rush of big swings drives your trading decisions then you are most likely going to lose it all at some point sooner or later.

There are plenty of other signs that your need for action is costing you money, as this list is not exhaustive. The best way to attack this problem is to monitor your behavior and pay attention to how you are feeling and what you are thinking when you are executing these trades.

"In the past week, what is the longest you have gone without checking your cryptocurrency wallet or brokerage account?"

Lesson 25 - Fight the FOMO

"Easy to feel left out in this kind of climate, seeing everyone on twitter going nuts over plays you are not in. Stay patient, don't let yourself get caught up in the emotion and stick to your plan. Be patient, be careful and chose your plays wisely."

FOMO stands for fear of missing out, and is something that is difficult for even the most veteran of traders to avoid.

FOMO messes up your entry point, starting the trade out on the wrong foot and often leading you to cut later for a loss. If all you are worried about is missing the opportunity in front of you rather than protecting your bankroll, then you have fallen victim to FOMO.

How does FOMO work? Imagine you have been having a really rough week of trading and are starting to get frustrated because all your trades are failing. You scan around your watch-list for new plays but can not find anything you like, and then all of a sudden your social media feed lights up. All your friends and the people you follow and respect online are talking about a play and how fast a play is running, and why they think it is going to keep running.

When you go to check the chart it is indeed looking bullish, and just had a fresh breakout a few minutes ago. You think about it for a minute or two but decide to avoid it, and then you look again and it us up another 10%. Now you are really wishing you had pulled the trigger, can not wait any longer and decide to FOMO in, but as soon you do it starts to go down.

"No reason to get all worked up and FOMO anything right now when there are a plethora of good setups available."

We all live for the thrill, we live for the action and when we see something moving that fast it really gets our attention. It is tempting to just blindly jump in, but in reality we should stay away because we have not done our homework.

It is hard to know why something is running so fast without researching, and by the time you research it the price has gone up even more. Sometimes it is a pump and dump scheme that is causing the move to happen, and other times a hot rumor that has everyone hyped up. When this happens you feel like you are forced to make a fast decision, and often times it is a bad one.

An often overlooked part of successful trading is doing proper research and studying charts ahead of time. For example, if you put in the time to scan your watch-list before the week starts, you will be in better position to capitalize on a good setup when it comes your away. In simpler terms, you will be prepped and ready for battle.

What does proper research look like? It is a multi step process, often involving examining the chart on different time frames, studying social media and reading the news to evaluate forward looking events. For each of us the exact way in which we arrive at our trade is a different, but without a doubt it should be a multi-factor analysis.

"When you hit that buy button are you excited? If so that is a sign of FOMO and emotional over involvement. You should be a cold calculated sniper, detached from the mission at hand."

One major problem that comes from FOMO is that your cost basis is out of whack. The price will normally move in a channel from over-sold to over-bought and when the price inevitably reverses after this pump you are likely to be underwater in your trade. Timing is everything, so if you buy in the middle to upper part of a pump you will be fighting against the tide trying to "fix" your bad trade.

Why is it so hard to resist FOMO? When you believe everyone else is making money you do not want to be left out of the party, as that can be lonely and depressing. This is especially the case when you have just had several big losses and are desperate to turn it all around with a big win.

"When everyone is super bullish and it seems like the price can't be stopped there is FOMO. Right now it's the opposite and it there is panic everywhere. What usually happens after these extremes?"

Lesson 26 - Dealing with Success

"Sometimes success is your worst enemy."

We have all read those articles about keeping your head up when things are going poorly, but what about when things are going great and it seems like you can't miss? That type of situation presents its own set of problems and they are rarely discussed.

In this article we will explore the practical lifestyle and psychological aspects of success, and how to stay on top once you get there. It most likely took you a long time to achieve this hard-fought success, so now that you are here let's talk about how to keep you on top of your game so you can enjoy the fruits of your labor.

It has often been said that the hardest part about trading is not learning how to read charts or how to analyze white papers or financial statements, but rather managing your own emotions. In this article we will explore some of the more common emotions that are associated with success, such as guilt, greed and over-confidence. Once you start to recognize the behaviors associated with these emotions you can begin to address them and cement your position as a winning trader.

"Do you feel guilty about your trading success when you see your friends struggling?"

One of the unfortunate side effects of success is the feeling of guilt, especially when you are a naturally compassionate person. If you started trading with a group of people, you may notice that many of those traders are still struggling, meanwhile you have learned from your mistakes and are now able to achieve a sense of financial freedom. In your favorite chat room or on twitter you see those same friends expressing their frustrations with the current price action, as you watch them repeat the same mistakes over and over again.

How does this sense of guilt play itself out?

Are some of your friends struggling so bad that they cannot pay their rent, phone or other bills? Do you find it hard to relate to them because you are doing so well and are flush with cash?

Perhaps you may find it awkward to talk to your friends about trading, and when you do you have to downplay your winning trades so they do not feel left out. These guilty feelings can also manifest themselves in other ways in your social life, for example when you go out to dinner or for drinks with your friends. Is there an awkward pause when the bill comes? Do you feel pressured to pick up the tab because you are doing well and they are not?

It would be entirely logical and perfectly human to feel guilty about your success if you are having any of these experiences. After all our friends and family are what it is all about at the end of the day. So how does one deal with those feelings of guilt?

If it makes you feel better to be generous and take your friends out to dinner once in a while that is fine, but you should by no means feel obligated to do so. You are successful because you have put in the time to learn, and have lived through the bad trading days/weeks/months/years to get to where you are now. You owe nothing to anyone else, and all your success is the result of your hard work. Never forget that.

"While these market moves are quite impressive it is important to stay grounded, otherwise you risk over reacting. Monitor your emotions and aim to be neither too high or too low - stay grounded."

If you are on a surefire winning streak, then one easy way to derail that train is to become over confident. Though confidence is not purely an emotion, it does have some emotional elements and they can get you into a lot of trouble.

You have to be hyper vigilant and follow all your rules closely, otherwise you will make costly mistakes. Hopefully these mistakes teach us incredibly valuable lessons, and as a side benefit can help to keep us humble. When you find yourself on a nice winning streak it is easy to get overconfident and forget what got you there: Strict adherence to trading rules. Over confidence can make you sloppy.

Another sure fire way to get in trouble is to become over-confident to the point of bragging to others about how well you are doing. The universe has a way of knowing when we stray too high or too low and pulls us back to the center where we belong. As the saying goes, pride comes before the fall and that is true for any trader who thinks that they are invincible to market forces or bankroll draw downs.

When you are bragging about your success to others, ask yourself if you are doing it to impress them or to impress yourself for some reason. Stop making yourself accountable to others, rather be accountable to yourself and your own goals. Let them live their lives and focus on living your own. In addition if you over sell your success to them, then you will have to keep up with the lifestyle and image you are presenting. This could lead to a lot of trouble if you hit a rough patch in your trading.

Trading is all about survival, so remember the long game and don't get too cocky. It has often been said that trading is a marathon and not a sprint, and that is absolutely true. The market can change a lot faster than you can adapt to it so you need to stay focused on surviving no matter what, which means you should still be careful even when you have been experiencing incredible success.

Stay grounded and keep reminding yourself what your goals were before you achieved success. If you can keep the bigger picture in mind, where you came from and what you need to keep going, then you are putting yourself in a good position to maintain your success.

"What goals do you have for yourself in the next 5 years, and how are you going to achieve them?"

Lesson 27 - Don't compare yourself to others

"Comparison is the death of joy - Don't get stressed or upset when you see another trader doing better than you. The only competition that matters is you against your own potential."

One sure fire recipe for disaster is combining the frustration of multiple losses in a row with comparing yourself to other traders. If you are down and out just remember that it is the bumps and bruises that we acquire along the road of learning that make us stronger. As discussed in other lessons, by following a disciplined rules-based strategy you can avoid those mistakes that make you want to quit, including comparing your results to other people.

People tend to react to other traders doing well based on their own character and life experience. Some are wise enough to use the success of others as a motivating factor rather than falling victim to envy, or having a "poor me" attitude. Always keep in mind that your personal trials and tribulations are all that matters practically speaking, not what someone else is doing or not doing on social media.

Even though we as traders may aspire to keep this enlightened view, it is tempting and in many ways natural to compare your own trading results to others: Especially the ones who are flashing big gains day in and day out. What you do not know is how many mistakes and bad trades they are making behind the scenes. As discussed in the social media lesson, this "guru" who is posting huge profits is probably only showing you the successful trades. The best people to follow on twitter and other social media platforms are the ones who make mistakes and are transparent as they try to learn from them.

Another critical reason is not to compare yourself to the guru you see flashing big stacks on social media is that they may have a completely different financial situation than you. This individual may be playing freely with their money and not really care what happens to it.

"It's money I can afford to lose so I don't even think about it."

There is a critical rule that you should never trade or invest any money that you cannot afford to lose. The people you see making huge profits on social media can probably afford to lose most or all of that money, but can you? If they are free to trade and invest without the emotional attachment to that money they are probably making less mistakes than you are.

Lifestyle differences are something important to consider as well when comparing yourself to another trader. You have no idea if the successful trader on social media is trading full time as a job or as a hobby. Full time traders have specific goals of how much money they need to make each week in order to pay their bills. These skilled traders know that they cannot afford to make big mistakes, so they stick to trading rules designed to keep them out of trouble. When you have to pay rent and your electric bill you are less likely to approach trading as a gambler taking casual risks.

Full time traders also have the time to watch the charts and follow their trades, whereas a part time trader or hobbyist may be making trades from their phone during a shift a work. This type of casual trading can be dangerous, and unless you are willing to buy and hold I would stay away from it.

Experience is also something to think about when you see that person on twitter making big money. They may have twenty years of experience and spend hours each night studying the charts or reading company financial statements. Is that what you are doing? There is no way to know what method someone goes through to prepare themselves to trade, as all you are seeing is the end result on twitter making you feel bad about yourself in comparison.

Unless you are working as hard as you can to prepare yourself each day for the new trading session, you will never know if you are working as hard as the person you see posting those big profits. Given this fact you might as well put in the time it takes to be ready for your trades, so that there is one less thing to worry about when comparing yourself to another trader.

Lastly, if you believe in your own technical analysis do yourself a favor and ignore other traders' charts. There is a reason I prefer not to comment on the work that other technical analysts do, and prefer to focus on my own work. One of the biggest mistakes you can make is to second guess yourself.

"Do not worry about what anyone else is doing. Trade your portfolio."

Lesson 28 - Scale in and scale out

"One bad trade can eliminate 10 good ones. Cut your losers early, and scale in properly to your position rather than at all once."

Managing your bankroll properly is critical to long term trading survival and success. One of the first things you should learn is how to scale in and scale out of your positions. What I recommend doing is taking the total amount you wish to deploy, and then divide that number by 3 or 4.

Take that first tranche and put it to work where you think a good entry will be, and then sit back and observe for a bit. If the price moves back up the way you expect it to and you receive some sort of trend changing confirmation then you can add to your position. If the price dips down further and you still think it is a good entry, then you can add to your position there as well.

When you fire all your bullets at once you are now at the mercy of whatever happens next, and no longer have the ability to react and adapt when new information comes your way.

This concept should also be applied to profit taking, as discussed earlier.

"Buying too early often leads to selling too late."

You must strike a balance with how quickly you double down or add a second or third tranche to your position. It is important not to add to your first buy too quickly, because if you do you will be in a tougher position should the price drop fast because you will be out of bullets. I recommend waiting for the price to visit a second key level such as an important resistance area, rather than just doubling down in the middle of the channel.

You can also wait for your position to be down a certain % before adding that second tranche, such as 25% or 30% depending on the market you are trading.

"If you scale in to your position rather than FOMO market buying the whole thing, your capitulation point might be your second or third entry. Capitulation is often a great entry point."

Lesson 29 - Self punishing

"Go easy on yourself. You can not learn without making mistakes, otherwise there is no lesson to draw upon. There is no shortcut to becoming a good trader."

Sometimes a mistake can be so bad that you think to yourself, "If I can just survive this one bad trade and get back to even, I'll learn my lesson." You tell yourself desperately that you will not make the mistake again, all the while you are hating yourself for getting stuck in that position once again. I know I have done this myself too many times to count. It happens immediately after making a repeated mistake and watching my position become more and more red with every refresh of the browser.

Holding onto losing trades in the hope that you "learn your lesson" is common form of self-punishment. Even as you know deep down inside that you should sell, you want to be stubborn and punish yourself by holding on to the trade. You tell yourself that maybe this time you will learn the lesson, thinking that if the loss is big enough you will feel the pain and not make the same mistake again.

The problem with that type of thinking is that once you emotionally recover from the loss, the same bad planning and desire to gamble will get you right back into trouble again unless you adjust your strategy. It is one thing to rebound emotionally from the loss, but it is another thing entirely to learn from the emotional pain and use that experience to change the behavior that led to the mistake in the first place. The desire for growth often comes from experiencing crushing portfolio losses, as it is a natural thing to want to avoid feeling that pain once again.

Another element of self punishment that we have touched on in other lessons is hating yourself for taking profit too early.

Have you ever had the experience where you make a really nice trade, or at least you initially thought so after scalping for a 10% gain? Once you sell you take your eyes off this play for a while and move on to other things, and do not look again for a few days. Then one morning you wake up and see that it ran another 35%.

After seeing the incredible move this stock has made you immediately feel terrible and start hating on yourself for taking profit too early. All for the rest of the day you make emotionally compromised decisions, as you are filled to the brim with frustration and self-doubt which ultimately ends up costing you money.

It is never a bad decision to take profit off the table, because you are defining your risk and locking up gains. If you want to avoid regretting future gains, then one good idea is to leave a small amount of your original position and let it ride.

"After any good run people take profit. At the top pumpers will tell you that's just "weak hands" and you should HODL. "Weak Hands" = strong bank account."

Lesson 30 - Trade with confidence

"Trade with confidence or don't trade at all."

If you are confident then you most likely lack fear because you know that your skills will help you navigate whatever the price action throws at you. You have been through it all and are not shaken when your long breaks support, as you know to wait for confirmation so you do not get faked out. You also know what a good opportunity looks like when it comes along and are confident in your ability to navigate that price action regardless of what happens.

"Study the chart ahead of time so you are ready no matter what scenario unfolds. Otherwise sit it out."

One great way to improve your confidence is to prepare ahead of time. If you are marking all the key price levels on the charts of your favorite plays then you will not get spooked out when volatility arrives.

But more than just skills and preparation, it is that you are operating with the proper bankroll strategy as well. As we touched upon in other sections, you really need to be playing with money you can afford to lose, because then you will not allow the fear of losing that money to interfere with making the right trading decision.

"Playing poker reminds me that you really have to not *need* the money in order to play the correct strategy. The minute you start thinking about losing X dollar amount, its over."

When you are continually trading from fear and weakness you are bound to make mistakes you would not normally make if you were trading from strength and confidence. Desperate to not lose another dollar, you become paralyzed and rather than seize on a good opportunity you hold back out of fear.

In order to play properly you need to have no fear of losing your money as long as the trading plan is solid and provides a good risk/reward setup.

"Fear of losing money is the #1 reason you are losing money."

Lesson 31 - Contrarian theory

"The simple formula for long term success is to buy when other people are unhappy about the price."

You have all probably seen that greed/fear indicator dial, where on the left side is fear and the right side is greed. There is a reason people track these things. When there is an over abundance of optimism and greed that often corresponds with a market top. The same is true when there is so much pessimism and fear about the price, often times a bottoming process is just around the corner.

"Clearly we are approaching a short term sentiment bottom - That would suggest to me a relief rally is just around the corner."

With this in mind you should try to find a way to monitor the sentiment of the market and your feelings when the price is fluctuating wildly. When you see the market participants starting to capitulate in large numbers, often times that shows up on social media and is hinting at an opportunity. It is often said that another person's capitulation is your nut bottom entry.

"Bottoms/tops can best be measured in sentiment, rather than technicals. As much as it pains me to say so being a chart guy."

Lesson 32 - Mind your trend lines

There are many important things to know about trend lines.

- Diagonal trend lines are more subjective than horizontal trend lines, so you are better off focusing on horizontals for your entry and stop loss levels.

- Trend lines can be drawn using both the candle body and wick. Japanese candlestick theory uses the body as it considers that the "essence" of the price movement. On the other hand classical charting patterns use the candle wick. Either are fine as long as you understand that it is more about the trend, rather than the line itself.

- A horizontal line by itself does not offer the same type of chart significance as several horizontal lines in the same area, which make up a zone.

- The steeper the trend line the more powerful it is, and the less sustainable it will be.

- The longer a trend line is in play (period of time) and the more times the price touches it, the more significant it will be if/when it is broken.

Of all these points, I think the most important is the difference between horizontal and diagonals, as well as the length of time and contact points so far as significance of any trend-line break.

Lesson 33 – Volume basics

Volume is one of the most misunderstood concepts in all of trading.

- The most volume typically comes at the top and the bottom of a chart, or at the start and the end of a trend. As discussed earlier once the trend in force meets resistance a volume filled battle ensues and the new trend takes over.

- Lack of volume is not necessarily a bad thing because a trend that is already moving does not need additional volume to continue in that direction. In addition almost every single consolidation pattern starts out with high volume, and then slowly trails off until the pattern completes.

- That being said, watch the volume on the red versus green candles. If the price is in an uptrend but the red candles have more volume than the green candles that is a warning sign. Always watch for contra trend volume.

"The lack of volume in the middle of the channel is a feature, not a bug. This might be one of the most misunderstood concepts in trading."

Lesson 34 - Indicator basics

Using technical indicators is a great way to gather extra information about the price action. This information can help you understand the trend and its momentum, and thus which direction the price may be heading. Let's look at some of the most common ones here:

- There are four types of indicators: Momentum, volatility, volume and trend.

- A momentum indicator is one that is used to determine the strength and weakness of a security by measuring the rate of rise or fall of prices. The most common one is RSI. RSI or Relative Strength Index measures a security's strength relative to its own price history, not the market itself. Computed on the candle close, the number oscillates from 0-100 with sub 30 marking over sold, and above 70 marking over bought.

- RSI also can have patterns similar to price charts, such as triangles, flags and head and shoulders patterns which can offer information about the trend.

- One thing to watch out for is a "failure swing", where the RSI leaves either sub 30 or above 70, and then after some consolidation an attempt is made to re-enter that zone and it fails. When that happens it is a clue of weakening trend strength similar to when you have a negative divergence.

- Next we have volume indicators, and my favorite the OBV or "On Balance Volume". OBV is also an index indicator, a tally of the buy volume versus the sell volume.

This is a great way to look at the strength of any trend, and to confirm when new highs are being made along with the price. Because OBV is not bounded the way RSI is, you can use it for regular divergence with confidence as discussed in a latter lesson.

- When prices are in a trading range and the OBV breaks support or resistance that can indicate the direction in which the price breakout will occur.

- One of the most common volatility indicators is the "Bollinger Bands". They are so important that I dedicated an entire lesson to them later. More or less, watch for them to squeeze in advance of volatility, and use the upper and lower bands as overbought/oversold and candlestick confluence.

- For trend indicators many chart technicians use the "ADX", or average directional index. The ADX is used by many trading systems as a tool to determine if something is up-trending or down-trending, as well as to determine the strength of the trend. Simply put it is a trend line that moves in a theoretical range from 0-50, bearish to bullish respectively.

With those basics out of the way here are some rules of thumb to remember when using these technical indicators.

- Oscillators can be bounded, or unbounded. Bounded means that it has an absolute limit up and down, such as RSI with 0 and 100 respectively. Unbounded oscillators do not have an upper or lower boundary, such as MACD, OBV or ADX.

- These indicators should never be used to generate a trade idea, but rather to confirm one. Simply put just because the RSI is sub 30 that does not mean a price bottom is coming, nor does it suggest you should open up a trade. Let the price action dictate how to risk your funds, based on momentum and interaction with key support and resistance levels, and then check the indicators to confirm your idea.

- It does not make sense to have multiple indicators that do the same thing. For example, you do not need to have OBV and A/D (accumulation distribution), or RSI and Stoch-RSI. Try to simplify your setup so that you can focus more on the candles and price action, and less on the many crossing signals these indicators offer us.

"...RSI, or any indicator in general is used to *confirm* a trade idea, not generate one."

Lesson 35 - Lesson on confirmation

Confirmation is a complicated topic because everyone wants to know how to avoid getting faked out. How do we "confirm" a move, or a breakout? Though it is a bit of an open question there are some things that you should know to help you with your style of trading.

- Percent or point filter: You can use a price movement of a certain % away from the breakout level as your confirmation. For example a 3% filter with a $100 breakout level, after $103 that breakout would be "confirmed" based on this method. One famous technical analyst Thomas Bulkowski calls the breakout a failure if it fails to move at least 5% in the direction of the breakout.

- Volume confirmation – With any breakout you would like to see the volume expand to confirm that break, indicating that the market players are putting funds to work in the direction of the trend. If that volume is missing you should be a little bit more suspicious about the break.

- Along these lines you also want to look for volatility to increase with the breakout as this would be a sign of increased interest and momentum. If volatility does not increase with the breakout, that raises the odds that it is false.

- Another way to think about a confirmation is with a "time filter". You can decide that as long as the price closes above the breakout level for X number of days, the breakout is confirmed. This type of filter is more useful for swing trading than quick flip trading as it is a conservative filter.

As I explained above there are many different ways to "confirm" a breakout, so it is really up to you and your playing style to determine what fits best.

Lesson 36 - Candlestick context matters

Japanese candlestick analysis should be part of any trading method, so here are some important things to keep in mind about my favorite type of analysis.

- Context matters. A bearish reversal candlestick signal is much more significant at the upper BB (strength evident) versus middle or lower BB (not as much strength). To put it simply a reversal candlestick needs a trend to reverse.

- All candlestick signals are short term signals and require follow through. For example a hammer or dragonfly doji at the lower BB is an excellent reversal signal, but it does not mean you are going to blast off for the next several sessions. Every candle requires confirmation, usually by closing above it in the next session and continuing with some type of substantial follow through in the direction of the trend.

- Looking at candlesticks without volume is useless. The strength of every candlestick signal is based on the volume behind it. For example after a downtrend a green hammer at the lower BB with strong volume is a much better indication buyer strength than a green hammer with light volume. Similarly, if you think about the "engulfing" patterns, you want the second candle (the engulfing one) to have at least 1.5x the volume of the first candle, to really show the change in momentum. An engulfing candle on weak volume is a weak signal and should be disregarded.

"Without exception, the strength of every candlestick signal needs to be judged based on the volume behind it. This is an immutable law."

Lesson 37 - Both sides of the trend

There are many things to understand about how trends form, continue in a direction and reverse.

- Technical analysis operates on the assumption of freely traded markets with prices that tend to travel in trends. Our primary job as technical analysts is to profit from riding that trend while watching for signs of weakening.

- Dow theory established the concept of "primary" (main) and "secondary" (corrective) trends. Always consider the primary trend when making your decision and diagnosing which level in the chart would signify a potential trend change.

- Trends are fractal, meaning that they exhibit the same behavior regardless of the time frame. Plainly speaking what that means is you can identify a bull flag on a weekly chart, but also on 5 minute or even 1 minute chart. With that in mind you want to remember that the longer the time frame the stronger the signal.

- Generally speaking trends tend to continue rather than reverse, which means in an kind of "jump ball" type scenario you should lean towards it resolving in the direction of the primary trend.

- When the price is trending it is moving in that a direction because there is an imbalance in supply and demand. Often times after a strong move the price will need to rest and move sideways while it digests the prior move. This type of action is normal as short term holders flip for profit and longs scale back while the indicators reset and prepare for the next leg higher.

- "The interaction of supply and demand is what determines the price, which means that however smart you think you are all that matters is where the buying and selling pressure show up on the chart. It does not matter if you think something is too cheap or too expensive, the market will make the ultimate decision. Don't argue with the price, rather respect it and trade accordingly."

- Always follow the trend rather than trying to fight it. I can not tell you how many times I have gotten in trouble in my early days of options trading trying to short a strong uptrend as soon as I saw one red shooting star candle. You want to be playing *with* the trend, so you should be looking to buy the dips rather than shorting the rips. Go with the trend not against it.

"Never argue with the market - it can stay irrational longer than you can stay solvent. Just follow the price action."

Lesson 38 - All divergences are not equal

Watching for divergence is an important part of any trading tool kit. Indicators such as RSI and especially OBV should confirm the trend, and when they do not we should become more cautious. With that in mind let's talk about the right way to use these indicators, and what you need to know about divergence.

- RSI (Relative strength index) is a "bounded" oscillator, which means it has an absolute limit for how high or low it can go. As such you should be careful using it for regular or reversal divergence. I recommend using RSI for "hidden" or continuation divergence, not regular.

- OBV (On Balance Volume) is an index indicator that measures the total red volume versus green volume, and is "unbound" which means it does not have an absolute limit up or down the way RSI does. Because of this fact OBV is a great choice to use for regular or reversal divergence.

- If you are a more conservative trader you can wait for "double divergence", where for example in the bearish scenario there are two higher highs with the price and two lower highs with the OBV.

- Lastly, keep in mind that the longer the trend has been in effect the more significant the divergence is.

The most important thing to remember from this lesson is that you should be careful using RSI for regular divergence, unless you are a professional. I recommend using OBV.

Lesson 39 - Principle of polarity

One of the most important things you will learn about technical analysis is the basics of supply and demand levels as expressed on the chart. When we think about support and resistance areas they are the level where the supply and demand for the underlying security has reached equilibrium and evens out. As discussed in an earlier lesson, this is why we find the most volume at the tops and bottoms of charts. Here is how to apply this knowledge in your trading practice.

- When a certain chart level has been tested and then rejected on multiple occasions with time in between those attempts, then you have a well established resistance or supply level. If eventually the bulls are able to break over that level and then eventually come back and re-test that level it should in theory be support. This is the principle of polarity. The same is true if you switch up the bulls and the bears in my scenario and multi tested support is broken, it will then turn in to resistance.

- When a broken resistance level of re-tested it is called a "throwback". When a broken support level is re-tested, it is called a "pullback".

- The more times a resistance or support area is tested, the more important it will be in the future. If that level is eventually broken, that break will carry more significance given how many times the price interacted with it.

There should be two big takeaways from this lesson. Firstly that the more a level is tested, the more significant its break will be. Secondly, that established support and resistance levels once broken will switch roles from resistance to support and vice-versa.

Lesson 40 - Common naming mistakes

There are a few basic mistakes that I see repeated over and over again in regards to naming chart patterns and basic price action so I figured I would take this opportunity to address them here. At the end of the day it does not matter what you call something as long as you trade it correctly, but you might as well know the correct terminology.

- "Back-test" vs "Re-test" – You have probably heard this many times where someone talks about a "back-test" of support. In reality they are talking about a "re-test" of support, because "back-testing" refers to testing an automated trading strategy against a set of historical data.

- Another common one is when someone notices some bullish consolidation and posts a chart on twitter pointing out a "bull flag". The only problem with this is that they have drawn a bull "pennant", not a "flag.

- A flag has two parallel lines that mark an upper and lower boundary, and normally is a falling channel or a correction in an uptrend. Normally this channel should not go longer than 50% of the length of the flag pole before breaking out. A pennant is comprised of two converging lines, the most commonly as a symmetrical triangle after an advance.

- With Japanese candlesticks I see people confusing a "doji" with a "spinning top" all the time.

- A doji is a candle session where the open and close are basically at the same price suggesting indecision. Sometimes you have a gravestone doji (bear), dragonfly doji (bull) or long-legged doji (neutral). With all candle signals the context depends on where this candle comes in the channel, vis a vis lower or upper BB for example. Keep in mind that in order to qualify as a doji the candle body must be no more than 5% of the entire candle range, otherwise it is a spinning top.

- A spinning top is a small real candle body, often expressing the same indecision as the doji but with a real candle body rather than a flat close versus open. Common examples of this are a hammer, shooting star and of course "high wave spinning top", the cousin of the long-legged doji. As with other candle signals context is extremely important. For example if you get a spinning top after a strong advance that reflects indecision in the market and a blunting of the prior bull force.

"The two most common mistakes I see people making in eastern and western technical analysis: Confusing Bull flag for Bull pennant Doji for Spinning top and vice versa."

Lesson 41 - Moving average basics

Moving averages should be a critical part of any trading strategy. So, what do you need to know about them?

- A moving average is simply put the average price of a security over a certain period of time. The moving average is used to smooth out the price action. It has many uses such as support, resistance, stop loss, and cross over signals among others.

- The two main types are exponential and simple. A simple moving average (MA or SMA) assigns equal weighting to each period in whatever length moving average you are using. For example a SMA 10 on the daily chart assigns an equal weight to each of the last 10 daily periods.

- An exponential moving average is one that adds weighting to the most recent period, with decreasing weighting for every session after that in the series. As a result of this the moving average is more sensitive to price movement and is often used as short term support, such as the EMA 8 or EMA 12. I often refer to the EMA 8 as "primary uptrend support".

Moving average crosses can be used to generate a signal, with some of the most common examples being the EMA 8 crossing the 34, 12 crossing the 26 or the MA 5 crossing the MA 15.

- Moving average crosses work best in trending markets, not sideways markets. As discussed previously a reversal candle needs a trend to reverse. Along those lines a moving average cross needs a trending market to cross and reverse from.

- Moving averages lag behind because they are based on past prices, so when looking at a moving average cross you want to consider price proximity to MA cross. For example if the EMA 8/34 are bull crossing but the price has already moved 20% in the last few sessions, then a good part of that bull signal is likely baked in. In theory you would like the price to be as close to that moving average cross as possible when it happens.

"Keep in mind proximity to price with MA crosses. The further away from the cross the price is at the time, the weaker the signal."

Lesson 42 - BB Basics

Bollinger bands, developed by John Bollinger are one the most popular and in my view important technical indicators. Bollinger bands, or "BBs" consist of a simple moving average (SMA 20), surrounded by an upper and lower band that reflects recent volatility. The more volatility there is in the market, the wider the bands area.

- 90% of price action happens in-between the upper and lower BB, so a price movement outside of the bands is "outside of the standard deviation". Though this in and of itself is not a buy or sell signal, it is a sign that one should be careful that the price may have become over extended in the short term.

- Where the price is trading in relation to the bands is a reflection of the inherent underlying strength. For example when the price is constantly trading near the lower BB that is a sign of persistent weakness. This factor allows us to use our Japanese candlestick signals more effectively due to the idea that a reversal candle/pattern needs a trend to reverse. Bearish reversal candlesticks/patterns work best at the upper BB versus lower, and vice-versa.

- Once those BBs get tight we have what many traders refer to as a "BB squeeze", or "BB pinch". During periods of price volatility these bands expand, and then once the price calms back down and trades in a range they tighten. Eventually they get so tight that the odds of an impending volatile move increase dramatically and traders can use that "pinch" to help time their trades.

"All you really need to make money is to learn how to read candlesticks and bollinger bands."

Lesson 43 - All gaps are not created equally

What is a gap, and must they all fill? A gap is an area on the chart where the price makes a rapid up or down move in closed session trading. For example stock X is moving up and closes at $100, and then the following session opens up at $105. Now you have a price gap from $100 to $105.

Not all gaps are created equally, so let's discuss the different types using the example above.

- Breakaway gap – Let us say for example that the major resistance in the example above was at $102, so when it closed at $100 and then opened up the next day at $105 you are "breaking away" from the resistance. This type of gap has a lesser chance to fill than a "common" or "measuring" gap which we will discuss next.

- Measuring, or Common gap – This gap happens in the middle of the run and is usually a small gap that is often filled within a few sessions.

- Exhaustion gap – This is a gap that usually fills as well and is found at the top of an uptrend. In this theoretical example the price has been churning along for a while and now the daily RSI is 93. The following day there is a big gap up and then slowly that gap fills, with the price continuing down after. This is the sign of a potential blow off top.

- Breakdown gap – Lastly we have the type of gap that

forms at the top of an uptrend, often after a long period of consolidation and then breakdown. Think about a strong uptrend that suddenly pauses and forms a sideways price movement like a rectangle for 10-14 sessions. After that last session the price gaps down and continues, forming a breakdown gap that is less likely to fill than a common gap.

Gaps are good for trading because often the upper or lower part of the gap can form as support or resistance and give you a solid thesis upon which to form a trade. Many times as well strong up-trends have big shake out days that somehow find a way to fill a lower gap before continuing higher. Those are the kind of entries I wait for.

Lesson 44 - Wait for the re-test

If you think you missed your entry just wait for the re-test. More times than not after a breakout the price likes to come back and re-test that broken resistance. Earlier in this book we talked about the concept of being patient and waiting for a good opportunity. In my experience the best entries come from a re-test of support, so let's dive in to the most common types of setups that use this strategy.

- A throwback is a bullish "re-test" (not "back-test") where the price breaks through resistance and then after a period of time comes back and re-tests that level. Throwbacks are my favorite type of trade setup because you are by definition buying weakness in an up-trending security. Be patient if the breakout already happened and instead wait for the price to come back and re-test that new support.

- A pull-back is the opposite of this. When the price breaks down through support, consolidates a bit and then comes back to and re-tests that level. This pull-back is a great spot to open up a short position, as you are shorting the mean reversion of a down-trending security. You might be tempted to start shorting if the price has already broken a key support, but if you are patient enough you might get an even better entry on that re-test.

- A hammer or a dragonfly doji are two great reversal candlesticks, especially when they appear at or below the lower BB and have more than usual volume behind them. These candlesticks often represent the reversing of a trend, but the problem is that if you wait to buy on the completion of the candle there has already been a decent bounce from the lows. Therefore you should wait for the price to consolidate a bit and it will likely come back and test the mid to lower part of that hammer or dragonfly doji candle range, offering an excellent risk/reward entry.

"Japanese candlestick theory -The best entries often come from re-test of reversal candle/pattern support."

Lesson 45 - How to set your target

People seem to ask me all the time, "What is your target?" and I respond by telling them to follow trends and not targets. In my view focusing on a target takes you away from observing the current price action where you will find clues about trend strength. There are reasons to use targets however such as setting some profit taking limit orders for unexpected price movements, or for calculating the risk/reward of any trade.

- Most targets are measured from the breakout price, the key level in the price consolidation that signifies a break and resumption or reversal of trend.

- Most consolidation patterns have a measured move or price target based on the height of the pattern, from initial lows to initial highs. For example with a symmetrical triangle you would take the widest point, and then extend that from the breakout point which is usually somewhere near the apex or cradle(most narrow point).

- In addition you can use major support or resistance areas as targets. For example if you break out of a lateral trading range and clear that lower high, then the next major price cluster or resistance/supply area should be your target.

- Another way of setting price targets is to use fibs or Fibbonaci retracement levels. Fibs are horizontal price levels that suggest where support and resistance should be. These levels are based on a certain % price retracement, such as 23.6%, 28.2%, 61.8% and 78.6%.

Price targets are helpful for setting profit taking orders, as well as keeping an eye on a potential upcoming trouble areas like a major resistance level. Use them wisely, but as I stated earlier I also think you should stay focused on the trend more than on targets.

Lesson 46 - Fasten your seat-belt

"The biggest difference between trading and gambling is a stop loss."

As discussed in other lessons already using a stop loss is critical to any successful trading approach. Let's talk about the different types of stop losses:

- Money stop – You can enter a trade and decide that you are willing to stick it out as long as you do not lose more than X dollar amount. So with a $500 position you may chose not to lose more than $50 for example. The problem with this strategy is that you are basing your stop on an arbitrary level when it should be based on a key price level or other metric.

- Percentage stop – This is a more common one where you decide to define your risk by saying that you are not willing to lose more than X% of your position. For example with a $100 position and 8% stop loss that would be $8. The drawback to this strategy is that it is also an arbitrary way to decide your stop, rather than upon a supply and demand area.

- A quite effective method for determining a stop loss is a key price level. On every chart there is a level that when captured likely signals a reversal in trend. If this is the case your stop loss should be just below or above that level depending on the direction of your trade, so that you allow your self a little room to work with in case of stop loss hunting.

- If none of these other methods work, then your stop loss should be based on your "thesis". The "thesis" is the reason you entered the trade, such as that it broke a resistance level, had building bull volume, or perhaps looked to test a key support level such as a multi year uptrend line. If the price now fails and does not hold that level then your "thesis" failed and you should exit your position immediately. Respect your thesis and that will help you from getting into too much trouble.

"Today is a great day to start taking your trading seriously. Have a plan (thesis) and respect your stop loss (risk). Respect your money."

- When you are setting your stop loss level your trade idea should offer at least 3 times the amount of profit you are willing to risk as a loss. Put simply a 3:1 profit to stop loss ratio.

- You should never move your stop loss away from the trend. That is if you are in a long trade and the price starts to come down, resist the urge to move your stop loss lower just to stay in the trade.

"Small losses are like calluses on your hands and feet, when they heal you are stronger and more durable. The big losses cut deepest so make sure to use a STOP LOSS."

Lesson 47 - Outside/Inside bars

You might have heard these terms before and wondered what they meant, so let's dig right in.

- An outside bar is a candle that completely eclipses the range of the prior candle. The high, low, open and close of the prior session all fall within the range of this "outside bar". What this means in practical terms is that the prior trend was challenged, and this outside bar is a reflection of that. When you see the outside bar you should take note that the trend may be stalling and stay on the look out for signs of further weakening. The outside bar often contains a bearish engulfing candlestick (candle body) as well, though it is not required.

- As a rule of thumb, when an outside bar closes near the low or the high of the session, it suggests further momentum to come in the direction of that close.

- On the flip side of that we have the "inside bar", where the entire range of that candle is contained within the range of the prior candle. The inside bar suggests a slowing momentum, with consolidation to come. Inside bars also represent a tightening range, often with two or even three inside bars in a row. Think of them as a clue that volatility is close by, and so you should be watching closely to see which way the price breaks.

"... Depends on how it breaks (the inside bar)."

Lesson 48 - Limit Order vs Market orders

You have probably heard these terms before: Limit order, market order, sell wall, prop bid and order book. Let's take a look at them now.

- When you are trying to enter a trade you have two options. You can place a limit order or a market order.

- A limit order is an order to buy or sell something at a certain price or better. For example if you want to buy $AAPL and it is currently trading at $123, you can set a limit order at $108.50 and if the price comes down to that level your order will fill.

- A market order is an order that buys or sells the security immediately at the current price. One problem with a market order is that sometimes there is not enough liquidity to fill your order at the current price, so you may get a less favorable order fill as you are subject to the market maker and available demand.

- As you are waiting to enter your trade via a limit order, the chances of you filling depend on where you place your trade in the order book. The order book, simply put, is a display of the buying demand and selling demand at each price level, posted for all market participants to see as they decide where to place their orders.

- In this order book sometimes people place a large sell order somewhere with the goal of intimidating buyers.

This is often referred to as a "loading wall", and it exists to help a large holder that wants to continue accumulating before the price goes higher. As a retail trader the normal psychological reaction is to fear this big sell wall in the order book, when in reality we should take note of it and perhaps study the price action a little bit closer.

- On the other end of the spectrum from this is a "prop bid", or buy wall. To the average retail trader this appears to be an eager whale, a big buyer that refuses to let the price go down below a certain level. When bears are in control this person is a hero to all the retail buyers, giving them the confidence to place their buy orders above this prop bid and usually they get filled. The only problem is that many times this is actually a big seller, using that prop bid to hold the price up while they unload their position.

"...That's actually bearish, I know it's counter-intuitive but it is bearish. This is called a "prop bid", and often will get pulled if it begins to fill. The opposite of this is a "loading wall", where you see a huge sell order, scaring others (retail) into selling."

Lesson 49 - Patterns rules of thumb

Classic charting patterns are fun to use, because they help us feel like we can understand what the price action is doing and that offers us clues as to which way the price will go next. Let's look at some of the most important things you need to know about using patterns.

- Patterns fall into two categories: Continuation and reversal. The most common continuation patterns are flags (bull/bear), pennants (bull/bear) and triangles (ascending, descending, and symmetrical).

- As with all other patterns these will start out with higher volume and then trail off until the pattern completes. Many traders see this lack of volume and mistake it for weakness when it is normal consolidation.

- Generally speaking shorter patterns are more common and less reliable as to the conviction of the pattern break. On the other side of that, the longer and more complex patterns are less frequent and more reliable. The best patterns are in the middle of frequency and complexity.

- Lastly the longer the time spent in a pattern digesting the prior move, the more important the price break of that pattern will be.

From this lesson I would suggest you pay attention the idea of continuation versus reversal plays. Focus your attention on those continuation plays, because you are going with the trend versus against it.

Lesson 50 - Relative strength

"During those key market moments scan through a list of your 8-10 favorite plays on the 15 minute chart and look for relative strength. Focus there to generate a better trade setup."

- When everything is pulling back and the market is showing weakness that is the time to start to watch for relative strength. In an environment of sell pressure across the board during some kind of market wide event it is worthwhile to see which ones are putting in higher lows, and which ones are not.

- Consider what was bullish before this across the board draw down. The charts that were bullish before hand had relative strength and are more likely to bottom than charts than had been lagging. Find the charts that have that relative strength and then prepare to position yourself there with a good trade idea and stop loss.

- The stronger charts will still have their price structure in tact after market wide corrections, so other traders will also spot that and that makes these plays more likely to continue.

"What has been hot is the best indicator of what will be hot."

Conclusion

Thank you for reading my book! I hope it helps you in your journey to become a better trader.

Cheds

Printed in Great Britain
by Amazon

63327470R00068